STAYING Healthy

By Selina Wood

Series Literacy Consultant
Dr Ros Fisher

Pearson Education Limited
Edinburgh Gate
Harlow
Essex CM20 2JE
England

www.longman.co.uk

ISBN 0 582 84145 3

Colour reproduction by Colourscan, Singapore
Printed and bound in China by Leo Paper Products Ltd.

The Publisher's policy is to use paper manufactured from sustainable forests.

10 9 8 7 6 5 4 3

The following people from **DK** have contributed to the development of this product:

Art Director Rachael Foster

Martin Wilson **Managing Art Editor** | **Managing Editor** Marie Greenwood
Polly Appleton **Design** | **Editorial** Selina Wood
Brenda Clynch **Picture Research** | **Production** Gordana Simakovic
Richard Czapnik, Andy Smith **Cover Design** | **DTP** David McDonald

Consultant Dr Cornelia Franz M.D.

Dorling Kindersley would like to thank: Anton Deans-Tahir, Jordan Du Maurier, Natasha Tiwari for their help and patience; Adam Allen, Hannah Burke, Anthony Deans-Tahir, Omar Deans-Tahir, Victoria Deans-Tahir, Beres Dowe, Lisa Du Maurier, Nabeela Malik, Josh Miller, Emma Newborough, Aneesha Tiwari and Shammi Tiwari for modelling and assistance; Gary Ombler for photography; Andy Crawford for additional photography; Alex Pang for illustration; Rose Horridge in the picture library; Johnny Pau for additional cover design work.

Picture Credits: Science Photo Library: Andrew Syred 24bl.

All other images: DK Dorling Kindersley © 2004. For further information see www.dkimages.com
Dorling Kindersley Ltd., 80 Strand, London WC2R ORL

Special thanks: National Asthma Campaign, Diabetes UK and Allergies UK; Langbourne Primary School, Chatham Grammar School for Girls and King's High School; Dr Buchanan, King's College Hospital, London; J Sainsbury plc; Crystal Palace National Sports Centre.

Contents

Staying Healthy

For most of us staying healthy is a matter of eating nutritious foods, exercising regularly and receiving proper medical care. For people with a chronic, or ongoing, disease such as diabetes, allergies or asthma, staying healthy involves taking steps to control their illness. A chronic illness is a disease or condition that does not go away and that currently has no cure. Most of these illnesses are controlled with diet, exercise and medication. This book takes a look at how three children live with either diabetes, allergies or asthma.

Asthma is a condition that affects the respiratory system. The airways, or **bronchial tubes**, narrow and make it difficult to breathe. Asthma attacks can be triggered by **allergens**, strenuous exercise and very cold or polluted air. About 150 million people around the world have asthma.

Jordan, age eleven, has asthma.

Footnote

Treatments differ from place to place and from person to person. The true stories presented here do not promote specific treatments, but they tell of these children's real experiences.

Allergies occur when your body has a negative reaction to something. People can be allergic to many different things. Foods, grass, pollen, dust and animal fur are common allergens. Reactions range from stuffy noses and itchy eyes to more serious effects, like severe breathlessness. Allergies to nuts are among the more serious allergies, and peanuts are responsible for most of the severe allergic reactions to food items.

Diabetes is a disease that prevents the body from processing glucose, or sugar, normally. There are a few types of diabetes. Type 1 and Type 2 diabetes are two common forms of this illness. About 177 million people in the world have diabetes, and the numbers are increasing.

Anton, age nine, has diabetes.

Natasha, age fourteen, has allergies.

Coping With Diabetes

Anton loves to play football with his friends and is a great swimmer. Anton also has Type 1 diabetes. This means that his body does not produce insulin, a **hormone** that turns glucose from food into **energy**.

Anton swimming

When Anton was two years old, his mother discovered that he was so thirsty that he had dragged a chair to the sink to drink straight from the tap. Up to this time, Anton had seemed to be a healthy little boy. Within a few days, however, he became weak and sleepy. He began to lose weight. He was also urinating often. His worried mother took him to the doctor.

After hearing the **symptoms**, the doctor immediately tested Anton's urine to measure the amount of glucose. Only a blood test could confirm a diabetes **diagnosis**, but the doctor knew that the level of glucose in the urine might point to the problem. The test showed a very high level of glucose in Anton's urine. His case was serious, so the doctor called for an ambulance to take Anton to the hospital. He stayed there for two weeks and was diagnosed with Type 1 diabetes.

Types of Diabetes

Type 1

- 5 to 10 per cent of all cases of diabetes
- appears mostly in young people
- usually develops quickly
- no insulin is produced – treatment requires insulin **injections**

Type 2

- 90 to 95 per cent of all cases of diabetes
- appears mostly in overweight adults, forty years and older
- usually develops slowly
- some insulin is produced – treatments include diet and exercise; some people need extra insulin

All-Important Insulin

In most people, insulin is produced in an organ called the pancreas. Insulin is an important hormone that controls the amount of glucose that flows in the blood. Anton's body doesn't produce any insulin because of his Type 1 diabetes, so he must receive insulin injections. Anton's mother gives him the first injection before he eats his breakfast and a second one before he eats dinner.

For Anton, injections are as regular as brushing his teeth. He has to follow a regular timetable for his meals and injections. After eating, the glucose from his food rushes into his bloodstream. The insulin keeps his blood glucose level from rising too high. On the other hand, if Anton doesn't have a meal after his injection, his blood glucose level can fall very low. Maintaining a balance between his diet and medication is an important part of Anton's day.

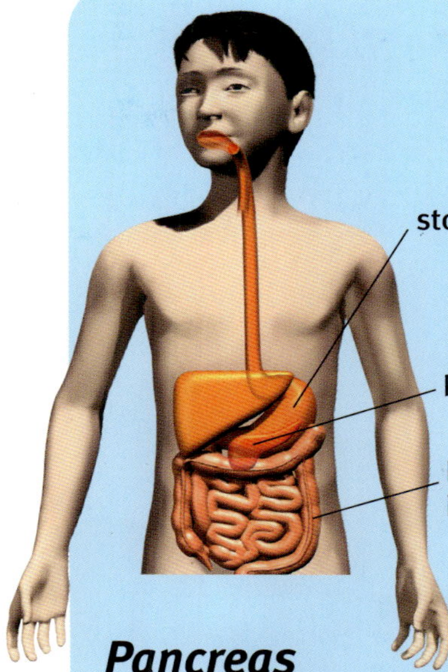

Pancreas

Insulin is made inside the pancreas. This is an organ found behind the stomach.

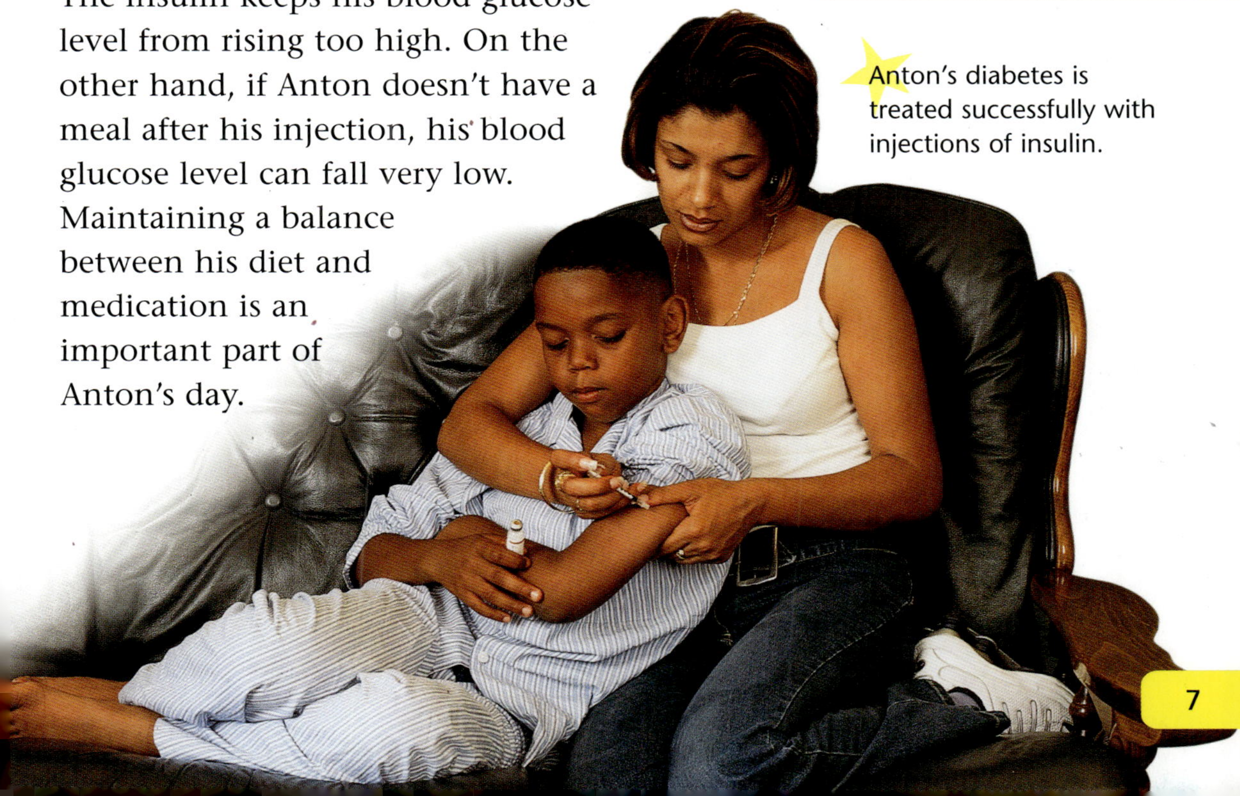

Anton's diabetes is treated successfully with injections of insulin.

Signs of Diabetes

- intense thirst and hunger
- frequent need to urinate
- feeling of tiredness
- weight loss
- blurry vision

Managing Diabetes

When Anton wakes up in the morning, he begins his day with a blood glucose level test, so that he knows how much insulin to inject. His mother uses a device with a needle in it to prick his finger. Then a small drop of Anton's blood is placed on a chemically treated strip of paper. A special machine "reads" the strip and shows how much glucose is present in Anton's blood. Regular glucose testing is important because both low and high glucose levels could cause problems. **Symptoms** of low glucose levels include sweating, nervousness, hunger and dizziness. Symptoms of high glucose levels include confusion and slurred speech.

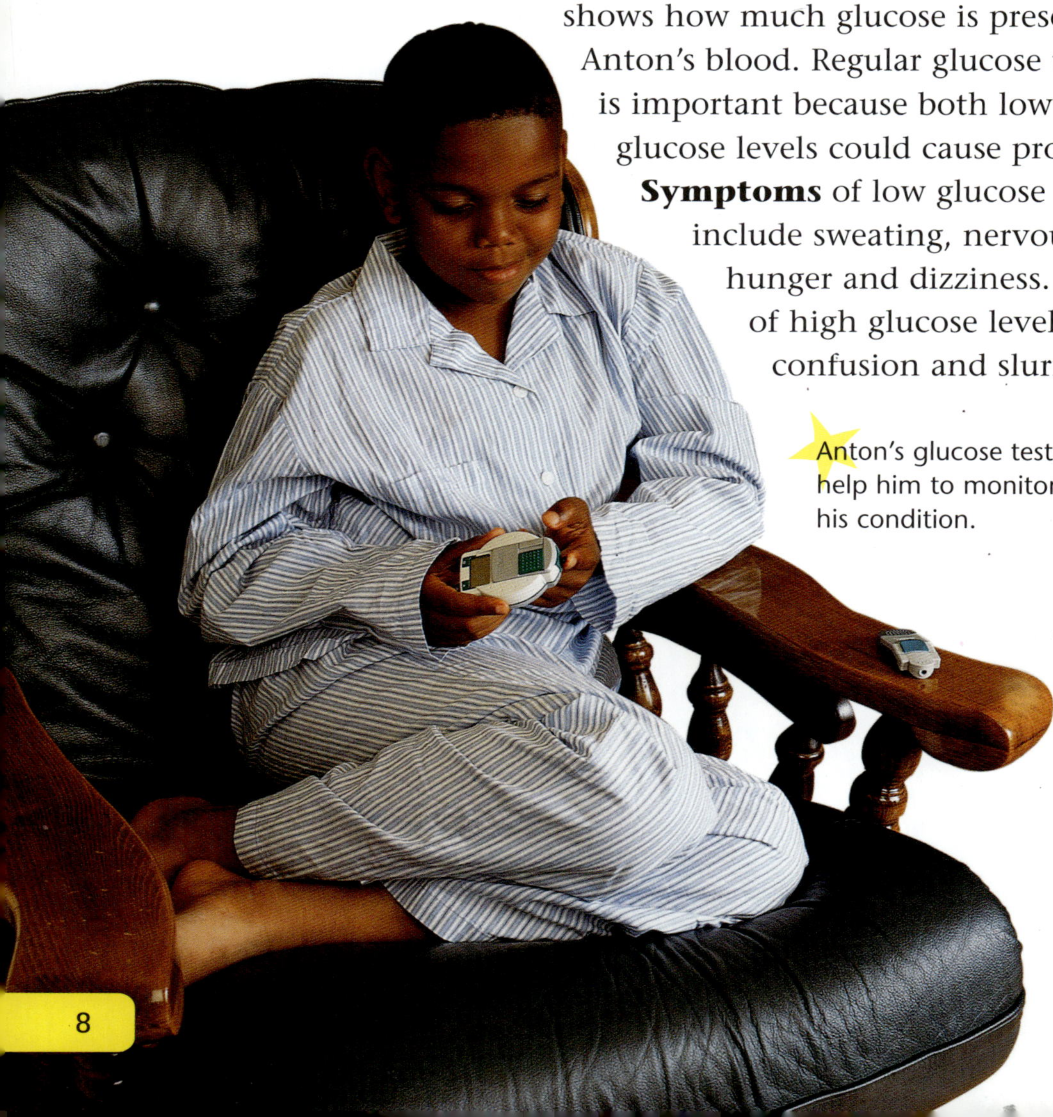

Anton's glucose tests help him to monitor his condition.

Anton's School Day

Anton's school day is very much like that of the other children. His favourite subject is design and technology, and he enjoys spending time with his friends. However, Anton must make sure that his glucose level remains in a healthy range throughout the day.

Since Anton takes his insulin **injections** regularly, his glucose level tends not to get too high, but he also must be careful not to let his level get too low. One way he does this is by having frequent snacks. During morning playtime, Anton usually eats some crisps. If he forgets, then his low glucose level makes him feel dizzy and he starts to shake. If this happens, then he must eat right away. He also carries glucose tablets with him at all times. Taking one gives him an immediate boost of sugar to help him feel better fast.

Anton enjoys climbing with his friends during playtime.

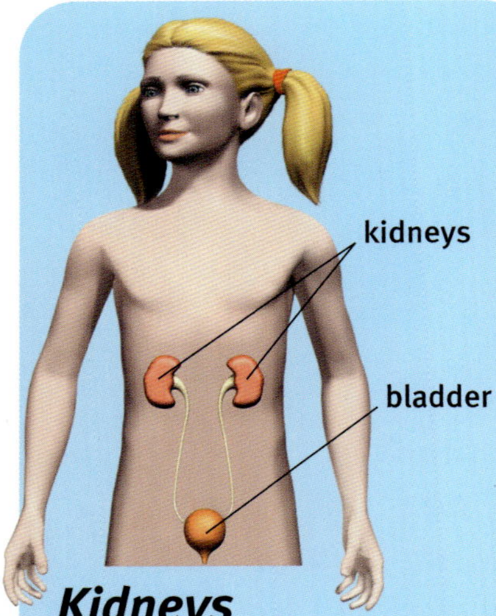

Kidneys

Why do people with untreated diabetes feel so thirsty and have to go to the toilet frequently? These **symptoms** occur when there is too much sugar in the blood. The kidneys try to filter out the sugar to keep the blood healthy. When the glucose level rises in the blood, the kidneys can't hold the extra glucose, and it ends up in the urine. Glucose must dissolve in water to leave the body, so the kidneys use lots of water to get rid of it. Thirst is the body's way of saying it needs this water, so a person with a high glucose level in the blood feels thirsty.

Anton also makes sure he eats a nutritious meal at lunch, usually some starchy foods, such as bread, potatoes or pasta, along with plenty of vegetables and some meat for protein. Together, these foods provide **energy** to help him feel well throughout his school day.

Anton can eat some sugar. However, he must be careful to make sure it is only a small amount. Anton developed good eating habits early because he had been diagnosed as a diabetic when he was very young. He knows some children his age who were diagnosed with diabetes later in life. Controlling their diet and trying not to eat sugary foods is difficult for them. Luckily for Anton, most of his friends have known him for a long time and know about his condition. They don't offer him things they know he can't eat.

Glucose comes from the digestion of starchy and sugary food, such as bread, rice, potatoes, yams and sweets.

Living With Diabetes

Anton likes many sports, but he is particularly good at swimming. His classmates bring a snack to eat after the swimming lesson because the exercise makes them hungry. For Anton, it is important to eat snacks both before and after the lesson. He usually eats a chocolate bar before strenuous exercise to stop his blood glucose level from falling too low.

Once every couple of months, Anton goes to the diabetes clinic, a special centre at his local hospital. The doctors check his weight, his glucose level, his kidneys and also his eyesight. A build-up of glucose can have a bad effect on the kidneys and can damage the eyes, leading to blindness. Anton's doctors help him make adjustments to his routine as his body grows and changes.

Anton loves swimming.

Anton doesn't mind going to the clinic because he meets other people with diabetes there. He likes talking to people who have the same condition.

When Anton comes home from school, his mother checks his glucose level again and makes sure he has a snack before he begins his homework. Then she prepares a healthy dinner for the family. Before Anton eats, he gets his second insulin **injection**.

Anton ends his day with another glucose test and a final bedtime snack. Anton usually sleeps well. Sometimes, though, he wakes up in the middle of the night feeling shaky. Then he has to eat something to raise his glucose level.

Exercising, healthy eating and maintaining his glucose level are becoming routine for Anton.

To keep up his active life, Anton has to remember to balance his diet, exercise, maintain his insulin needs and listen to the signals he receives from his body. Once, while at a friend's birthday party, his mother was busy and Anton was enjoying himself so much that he missed his insulin injection. He had to take it as soon as he remembered. Another time, his mother was held up in traffic and wasn't there to give Anton his evening injection. His friend's mother had to give it to him instead, while Anton's mother gave her instructions over the phone.

Currently, there isn't a cure for diabetes, but that doesn't stop Anton from being positive about the future. He knows that a cure could be discovered at any time. Anton dreams of skydiving one day. He knows that having diabetes will not stop him from achieving his goals.

A healthy, well-balanced diet is good for Anton and his family.

Living With a Nut Allergy

Fourteen-year-old Natasha loves shopping, reading and going to the cinema with her friends. Natasha is also allergic to many different things including house dust, pollen and certain pets. She gets hay fever (an allergy to pollen) in the summer. She has also suffered from a skin rash called eczema since she was two years old. Natasha's most serious allergy is to nuts. Yet Natasha has learned how to manage her allergies from day-to-day.

What Causes Allergies?

No one is sure why some people develop allergies. Below is a list of ideas some scientists have that explain why some people get allergies.

- Allergies may run in families.
- Allergies may be caused by a virus.
- Environmental changes may lead to more allergies.
- We might be more sensitive to **allergens** because we live in a cleaner world.

Natasha's favourite breakfast is a bowl of fresh fruit.

A First Diagnosis

Natasha was only five years old when she had her first major reaction to nuts. She had a new breakfast cereal, which contained nuts, and went off to school. After an hour or so, she began to feel sick. Her face became swollen, her lips were tingling and it was difficult for her to breathe because her throat was swelling up. Natasha was rushed to the hospital and lost consciousness soon after arriving there. A team of doctors and nurses started to revive her. They were about to give her an **injection** of **adrenaline** when she came around.

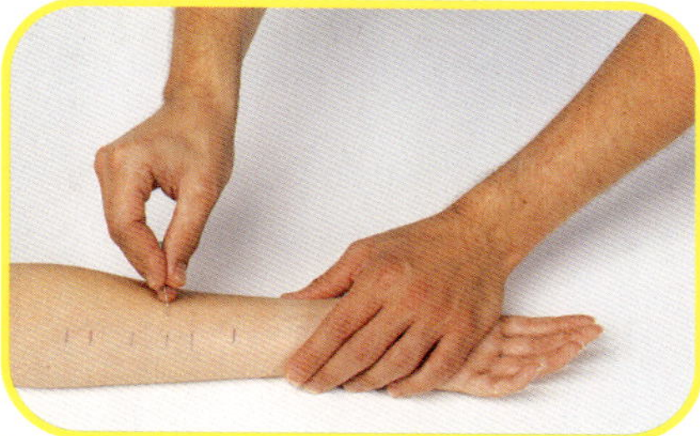

During a skin test, the doctor scratches a tiny drop of allergen onto the skin with a special device.

Doctors told Natasha and her mother that she had experienced a severe, life-threatening allergic reaction. The doctors traced her allergy to the nuts in her cereal. They told Natasha to avoid eating nuts in the future. That meant she had to check the ingredients of everything she ate which is often difficult. The doctors made some additional tests on her skin and discovered that she was allergic to many things.

Allergy to nuts is increasingly common.

Some Symptoms of Allergic Reactions

- swollen face, lips and tongue
- difficulty breathing
- itchy, red rash
- light-headedness, sometimes unconsciousness

Controlling the Allergens

Natasha's reactions to nuts can be life-threatening. As a result, she must carry medicine with her in case of an emergency. Natasha's doctors have trained her in how to recognize the **symptoms** of an attack and how to use the medicine in her pack.

If Natasha feels an allergic reaction coming on, she takes an antihistamine tablet, which blocks her body's allergic response. If she has difficulty breathing, she uses an **inhaler** to help her breathe more easily. If the attack is severe and won't stop, she uses an Epi-Pen™ – an auto-injector for life-threatening allergic reactions – to inject herself with **adrenaline**. Adrenaline increases the blood flow through the body and flushes the allergens from her system. If she develops a skin rash, then she applies cream to the affected area. Natasha also wears a bracelet to let people know about her allergies in case she passes out.

Natasha wears a medical-alert bracelet.

Mast Cell

Mast cells are found in the skin, nose and other areas of the body. The first time the body's mast cells are exposed to an **allergen**, they build up **antibodies**.

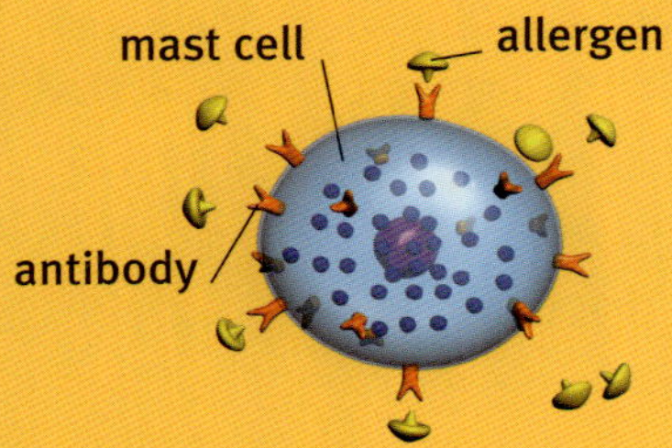

1. Antibodies produced during the cell's first exposure to allergens attach to the surface of the cell.

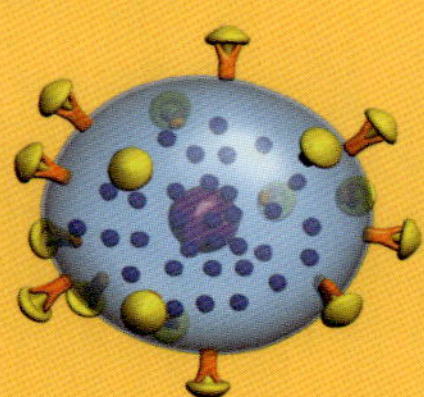

2. Allergens come in contact with antibodies during later exposure.

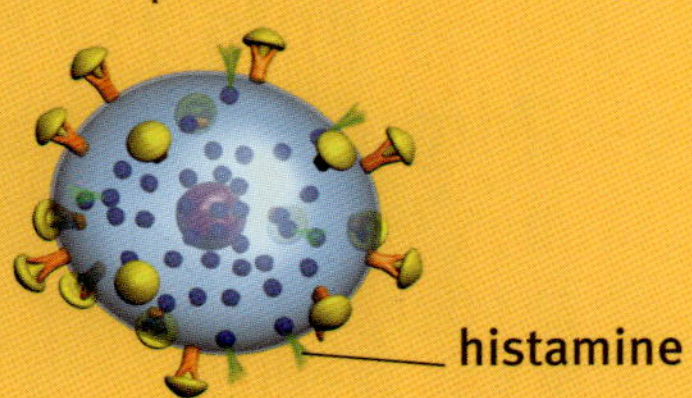

3. The contact of allergens with antibodies causes the cell to release histamine, producing an allergic reaction.

Natasha at the age of five

Natasha's School Day

On a typical morning, Natasha has a healthy breakfast and gets ready for school. Some mornings she feels the effects of her allergies, especially as spring comes and the amount of pollen in the air increases. If she notices her body giving her signals, such as itchy eyes, congestion or headache she takes allergy medicine. Then, just before leaving the house she checks her emergency medical pack, which she carries everywhere she goes.

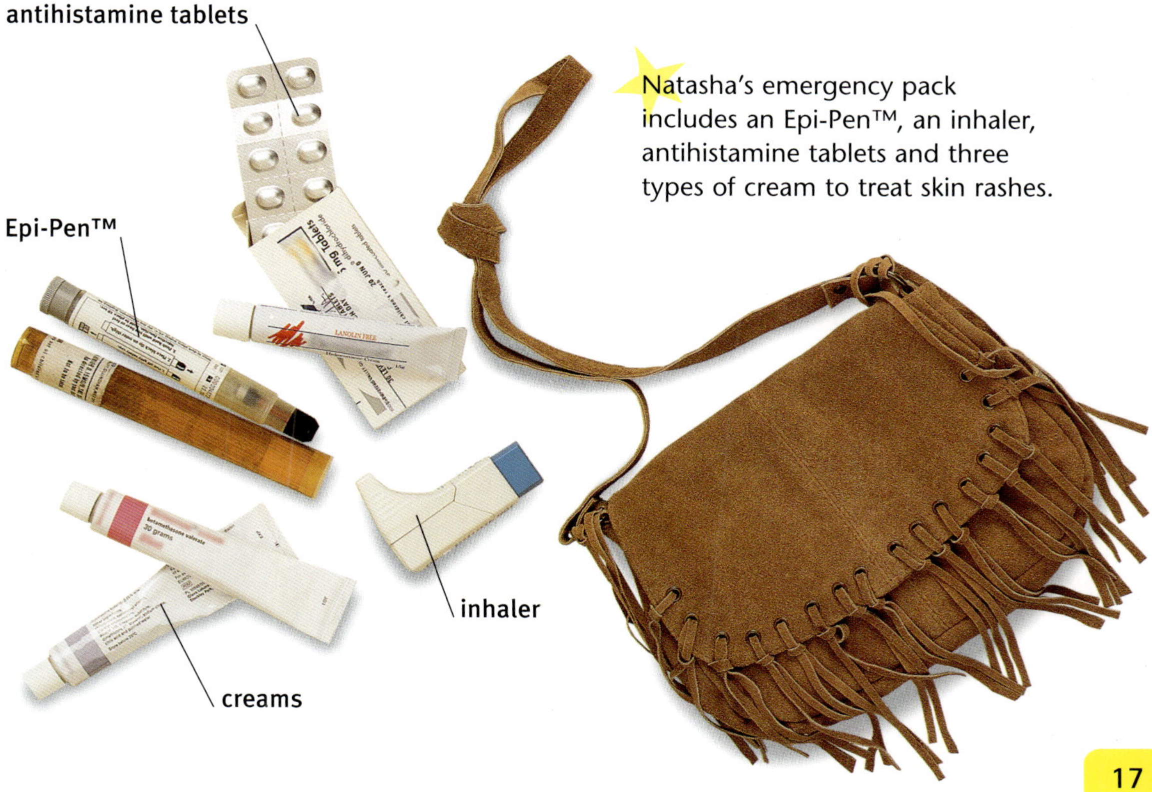

Natasha's emergency pack includes an Epi-Pen™, an inhaler, antihistamine tablets and three types of cream to treat skin rashes.

Allergy	Symptoms	Allergen
hay fever	runny nose, itchy eyes	pollen
eczema	itchy, reddened skin	dust mites, stress, pets, chemicals, detergents
asthma	wheezing, difficulty breathing	dust mites, pollen, mould, pets, tobacco smoke, certain medicines, exercise, stress, cold air
food allergies	swelling of the lips, hives, digestion problems, dizziness, sometimes unconsciousness	certain foods
bee/wasp sting	red rash, asthma, dizziness, sometimes unconsciousness	bee or wasp sting

Natasha studies hard, especially when it is time for exams. For lunch, Natasha eats with her friends in the school lunchroom. She checks with the dinner ladies to make sure that no nuts are in the meal that she wants to eat. She usually has pizza or pasta. Three other students at her school have nut allergies, so the school is well prepared.

Natasha chats with her friends during the lunch hour.

After school, Natasha loves to go shopping with her mother and younger sister. Sometimes they stop for a snack. When Natasha eats out, she always asks the waiter what ingredients are in the food before she orders from the menu and keeps the emergency kit handy, just in case.

Natasha also carefully reads the labels on other items, such as shampoo and beauty products. These items sometimes contain nuts or oils from nuts. If Natasha decides to wear make-up in the future, she will also need to check those labels. Several kinds of lipstick use nut oil. Fortunately, now many companies have labels warning people that nut ingredients are used in their products.

Natasha looks at the ingredients of things she buys – including shampoo.

At the weekend, Natasha spends time with her friends. She always makes sure to put her medicines into her handbag before going out.

Wherever she goes with her friends, Natasha must be aware of the food being served. If nuts are present, then she must be very careful. Natasha's nut allergy is so severe that she may have a reaction just from having physical contact with people who have eaten nuts. At a party a few years ago, she hugged and kissed her relatives who had been eating peanuts, and she had a bad reaction. Now she is very careful all the time.

When Natasha gets ready to go out, she puts her medical kit into her bag.

Natasha enjoys hiking trips with her friends.

Natasha enjoys hiking and camping. Once, when she was out hiking with friends they all stopped for lunch under a tree. Halfway through lunch, someone noticed that the tree they were resting under was a horse chestnut – a type of nut tree. The whole group got up and ran away! Natasha was okay, though. She didn't have an allergic reaction that time.

Nut allergies are lifelong problems. However, Natasha has learned to live with her condition and to avoid eating nuts. Her allergies don't affect her most of the time, and she has learned to read the warning signs her body gives her about a possible problem. Natasha successfully manages her allergies by being aware of her surroundings, paying attention to the food she eats and the products she uses, and by staying prepared in case of an emergency.

Symptoms of Asthma

- wheezing
- shortness of breath
- difficulty inhaling and exhaling
- coughing
- sweating

Kicking Asthma

Jordan is eleven years old. He has a passion for martial arts and enjoys kickboxing. He has even won a large collection of trophies in martial arts competitions and for running. However, Jordan is different from other competitors as he has asthma.

When a person has asthma, the air passages inside the lungs become irritated and swollen. When the passages swell, the airways become narrower, making it hard to breathe. Some of the **symptoms** during an asthma attack include coughing, shortness of breath, a tight feeling in the chest and wheezing.

Jordan has won more than thirty trophies for martial arts and running.

Managing Asthma

When Jordan was seven, he ran out of breath while running. He had always been very energetic, but suddenly he couldn't run because he felt his chest tighten up and he couldn't breathe. He couldn't perform in sports as well as he used to, so he felt very frustrated. Soon, each time he caught a cold, he noticed that he had trouble breathing.

After an asthma attack at school, Jordan was sent to the hospital. The doctor put him on a nebuliser, a machine that allows a liquid medicine to be inhaled as a mist. This relaxes and widens the airways and relieves symptoms. The doctor also gave him a medicine to reduce the swelling of his airways. This was the first step in managing Jordan's asthma.

What Is Asthma?

Asthma is a long-term chronic condition that affects the lungs.

- The airways are narrowed and inflamed.
- The inflamed airways produce too much mucus – a protective liquid that coats the inner lining of the airways.
- The airways are over-sensitive to many different triggers.

Normal Airway

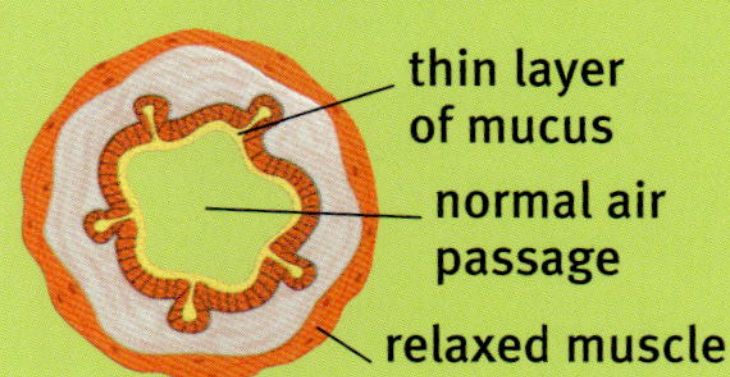

Constricted Airway

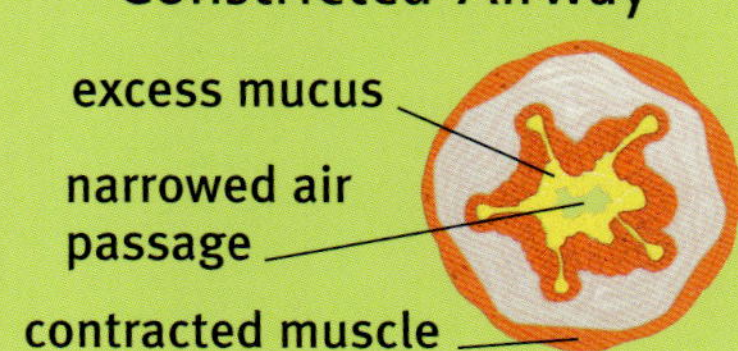

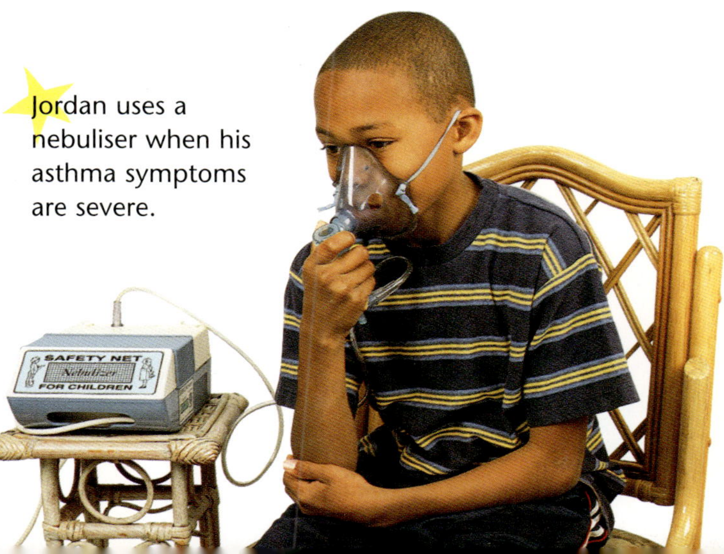

Jordan uses a nebuliser when his asthma symptoms are severe.

Jordan's School Day

Jordan starts the day with a puff from his **inhaler**. This helps to keep his airways relaxed and open and to avoid an asthma attack during the day. Unfortunately, it doesn't guarantee that he will not experience problems from his asthma, especially when the weather is cold.

Cold air is one of the things that can trigger asthma. Jordan must be especially careful during the coldest times of the year. He has to use a different inhaler and to use it more often. This inhaler has a reliever drug which relaxes the muscles around his airways and helps him breathe properly. Jordan makes sure to have his relief inhaler with him all the time.

What Causes Asthma?

Asthma tends to run in families, but the triggers and intensity of the attacks vary from person to person. Air pollution, cigarette smoke, perfume or dust mites can trigger off asthma attacks. It may also be triggered by the excess mucus produced during a cold or viral infection.

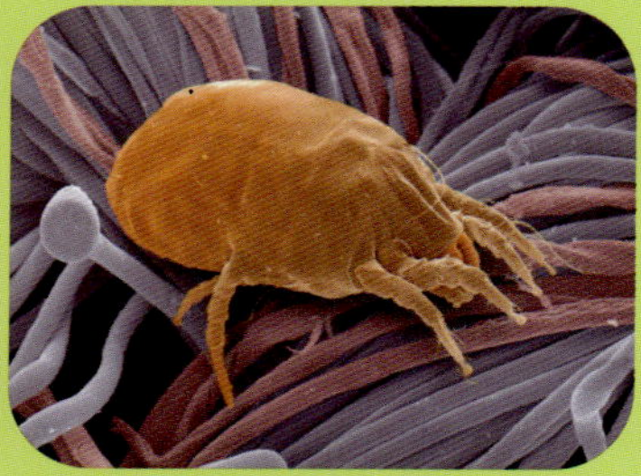

This dust mite has been magnified many times because a dust mite cannot be seen with the naked eye.

Jordan uses his relief inhaler.

Jordan takes many different classes, but he really loves science. He does not have to follow a special diet, so he eats whatever he likes at lunch time. Jordan knows what it feels like when he begins to have an asthma attack, so by listening to signals from his body, he can stop a serious attack.

Jordan really enjoys spending time with his friends and playing sports.

Jordan conducts science experiments at school.

After his **diagnosis**, Jordan used to sit on the sidelines while his friends played football because he was worried that he wouldn't be able to breathe. He also felt worried about using his **inhaler** in front of his friends. Then one day he went to see a former world champion kickboxer at his local sports centre.

Jordan is a champion kickboxer.

After hearing the kickboxer speak, Jordan decided to find out how he could play sports while managing his asthma. Jordan talked to his doctor and made a plan for dealing with his **symptoms** while exercising. Then he decided to take up martial arts. Since then, he has also taken up kickboxing and even cross-country running.

Jordan practises his martial arts.

Communicating With the Doctor

It is important for asthma patients to talk to their doctors. Patients need to discuss how to deal with their symptoms. Here are some ways patients work with their doctors.

- They ask questions and express their concerns about their condition.
- They tell the doctor about their goals and ask for advice on the healthiest, safest ways to achieve them.
- They keep notes of any symptoms or problems and share that information with the doctor.

After school, Jordan goes to martial arts practice. He also frequently competes in tournaments. During a tournament, Jordan faces several opponents. Matches are held in a large gymnasium with an audience cheering him on. Jordan makes sure that he follows his special routines to stay healthy during the match.

Jordan blows air into a machine called a peak flow meter before he competes. This device measures the rate of air that comes out of his lungs. Jordan uses this information to work out whether or not his lungs are working well. Normally, Jordan's air-flow reading is well above average because he is so fit from all of his sports training. However, he often finds his reading is only average before a competition because he is nervous.

About fifteen minutes before his first competition, Jordan usually takes a puff from his **inhaler**. This stops him wheezing and helps keep his chest from feeling tight. Sometimes Jordan feels asthma **symptoms** coming on in the middle of a tournament. If this happens, Jordan takes a few puffs from his inhaler. Within a few minutes, he can breathe normally again.

A peak flow meter can be used to measure Jordan's breathing capacity.

Jordan runs in a cross-country event.

Jordan won't let his asthma get in the way of his passion for sports. In fact, the more exercise he does, the less he needs his inhalers. He follows his doctor's advice, and has learned to listen to the signals he receives from his body. Jordan also no longer feels self-conscious about his inhaler.

Jordan's love of sports has given him the courage to learn to manage his asthma. He has won sports scholarships, and has run more than 5 kilometres in 18 minutes. Now his ambition is to appear in films – preferably martial arts films. Jordan really has given asthma a kung fu chop!

Jordan with one of his many trophies.

Conclusion

Living with a chronic condition such as diabetes, allergies or asthma does not have to mean giving up exciting opportunities. Anton, Natasha and Jordan face challenges with their health. They each prove that with education, good health care and supportive families, they can manage their conditions successfully.

These children show us how important it is to keep a positive attitude and to stay strong. Even when things are difficult or uncomfortable, they have found ways to meet the challenges they face. They are determined to manage their illnesses and to stay healthy.

Jordan, Anton and Natasha have great plans for the future.

Glossary

adrenaline a hormone produced by the body at times of stress or excitement that makes the heart pump blood through the body faster; it may be injected into the body to revive someone who is unconscious

allergens substances that produce an allergic reaction

antibodies special proteins in the body made by white blood cells that fight germs and other foreign substances

bronchial tubes tubes that branch off from a larger airway called the trachea and go deep into each lung

diagnosis a decision about a patient's disease that is formed after checking symptoms and taking tests

energy the body's fuel needed for action

hormone a substance produced by the body to have an effect on other parts of the body (such as to start growth or to control glucose level)

inhaler an instrument used for breathing in medicine

injections medicines forced into the body with syringes

symptoms bodily reactions that indicate a disease

Index